THE
ART
OF
/NSTIGATING

TOM MORKES

For Courtney; for making me practice what I preach.

TABLE OF CONTENTS

A PREFACE

THIS IS A BOOK ABOUT STARTING.

THIS IS A BOOK ABOUT BRINGING AN IDEA TO LIFE (ANY IDEA, AND IN WHATEVER FORM YOU CHOOSE).

THIS IS A BOOK ABOUT DOING THE SCARY THING THAT OTHERS WON'T.

THIS IS A SHORT READ. WITH ABOUT 70 PAGES OF CONTENT, YOU CAN READ IT IN ONE SITTING.

THIS IS THE CULMINATING EFFORT OF OVER 10 YEARS OF READING, RESEARCH, STUDY, TESTING, BREAKING, AND BUILDING.

THIS IS A BOOK LIKE ANY OTHER – TO REMIND YOU WHAT YOU ALREADY KNOW IS TRUE.

PART I :
HIT THE
SHORE

READY?

Before we start, I'd be remiss not to let you in on a secret:

YOU WILL FAIL.

Good, now that that's out of the way, we can get started.

A QUESTION

What do you want to create?

If you could build anything, start anything, lead anything, what would it be?

> **"MAN IS MADE OR UNMADE BY HIMSELF"**
> James Allen

INADVISABLE ACTION

Instigate: \ˈin(t)-stə-ˌgāt\

> "TO BRING ABOUT OR INITIATE
> AN ACTION OR EVENT. TO URGE ON TO
> SOME DRASTIC OR INADVISABLE ACTION."

Starting something from scratch; changing directions; building something without permission; moving, exploring and testing without a team of bosses telling you where to go and how to do it.

All of these are forms of instigating.

Instigating is about going off on your own, without orders, and making something happen.

It's about doing something that is scary and uncertain.

Instigating is about doing the inadvisable.

> "NO EXCELLENT SOUL IS EXEMPT
> FROM A MIXTURE OF MADNESS."
> Aristotle

THE ART OF INSTIGATING DEFINED

The *Art of Instigating* is both a **method** (there are steps) and a **practice** (you do it more than once) for creating, making, building, breaking, testing, and conquering.

Instigating is the **essential practice** of every great creator, and at the **core** of every successful venture.

It's about taking an idea and turning it into reality.

It's about making the ephemeral tangible.

There is beauty, strength and power in instigating.

But it's not easy.

If you've ever tried creating anything – a book, movie, blog, business, gang, whatever – you understand the pain of instigating: from coming up with an idea, to pushing through inertia to begin the project, to the grueling months (sometimes years) of development, to the final (terrifying) ship date – every step along the way is a possible stopping point, failure point, or breaking point.

It takes guts to create something without permission.

THE STAGES OF INSTIGATING

There is a method to the madness of instigating.

Stage 1) Start

The first stage of instigating is making the immaterial tangible; from idea, to spoken words, to written plans, to the first actionable step to bring your dreams to life.

Starting takes *vision*, *guts*, and *commitment*.

> ## "IF THERE'S NO ONE STARTING STUFF, THEN WHERE DOES INNOVATION COME FROM?"
> Poke the Box

Stage 2) Finish

The second stage of instigating is everything that follows that first actionable step to the completed product. Once you put that first word down on that piece of paper, now you're in the finishing stage. This can take days, weeks or even years.

Finishing takes *discipline* and *grit*.

> ## "IT'S NOT THE WRITING PART THAT'S HARD. WHAT'S HARD IS SITTING DOWN TO WRITE."
> The War of Art

Stage 3) Ship

The third stage of instigating is shipping the product to market.

This is very much different than finishing.

Finishing means the .pdf is saved on your hard drive; *shipping* is the final copy for sale on Amazon. *Finishing* means putting the branding on the box, *shipping* means fulfilling the order. *Finishing* means there's a calendar date set for the meet-up, *shipping* means you've gone door to door to shape the political landscape.

Shipping takes *courage*.

> ## "THERE IS ONLY ONE WAY TO FIND OUT IF YOUR PRODUCT IS GOOD, AND THAT IS TO START SELLING IT."
> The Reluctant Entrepreneur

Don't be fooled by the simplicity of these stages.

Each stage is essential. Nothing ships (intersects with the market) if it hasn't been created, and it can't be created until it's been thought of and built.

Common sense, not necessarily common practice.

> **"IF YOU ARE OUT TO DESCRIBE THE TRUTH, LEAVE ELEGANCE TO THE TAILOR."**
> Albert Einstein

LEARNING TO INSTIGATE

Instigating is a lost art.

All the greatest writers, painters, warriors, leaders, inventors, explorers, builders, creators and innovators throughout history understood instigation.

They understood how to **harness its power** and how to **apply** it in productive, fruitful endeavors.

These great men and women – the ones who mastered the *Art of Instigating* – are the people whose books we read, in whose buildings we work, whose art we hang on our walls, and in whose nations we grow, communicate, and thrive.

They mastered the *Art of Instigating* and *brought* to life the things that now *shape* our lives.

Anyone can learn to instigate.

By paying attention to the simple lessons in this book, you will come to understand the *Art of Instigating* and be able to apply it in your own life.

If you do that, the results will be life transforming.

It really is that simple. It's just not easy.

THE STAKES

The *Art of Instigating* is important because **your ideas** are important – and because **bringing them to life** means *everything*:

Learning and applying the *Art of Instigating* is the difference between success and failure.

It's the difference between pride in your completed work, and the intense guilt of wasted years and nothing to show for it.

It's the difference between being the incredible person you dreamed you could become, and the mediocre person you ended up becoming.

If you're an entrepreneur, it's the difference between building a business that you love and losing your mind one 60 hour workweek at a time.

If you're a writer, it's the difference between walking into Barnes and Noble to see a book with your name on it, front and center in the store, and reading the lackluster words of a stranger whose idea you had years ago, if only you had started...

It means everything because *your* dreams, *your* desire, *your* work, and *your* effort mean everything.

Will you write the book you've always wanted to write, build the business you've longed to build, or create and lead the organization you know the world needs?

Don't be another victim of "I'll start tomorrow."

Start today.

THE MOST IMPORTANT REASON TO INSTIGATE

There's one other reason (the most important reason) learning the *Art of Instigating* is so important.

By learning and applying the *Art of Instigating*, we set in motion the *progressive realization of a goal*; something we didn't think was possible - something that began only as a whisper in our minds and that now sits before us, fully realized.

When we bring that whisper to life, we recognize the most important thing in this world: **where there is desire met with effort, anything is possible.**

In the seemingly insignificant act of starting, finishing, and shipping, we harness the power of the human spirit and the infinite power that feeds us.

By *choice* we can create something from (almost) nothing, which is to say, in essence, we have actualized *freedom*.

Instigating, therefore, is about *freedom* (the ability to choose what we want and to make it a reality). It's about becoming our potential; it's about living our purpose; it's about the beauty of creation.

It is possible to live a life without instigating. There are many that do. Sadly, these people have never experienced the purity of freedom afforded to every conscious mind.

If there is something more you want out of life; an intense desire for something greater; a quiet whisper in your mind…

I'm asking you: bring it to life.

Do it for *yourself*.

Do it *for all of us*.

> **"PEOPLE THAT ARE FIGHTING FOR THEIR FREEDOM ALWAYS ULTIMATELY ACHIEVE THEIR AIM."**
> The War of the Flea

INSTIGATOR VS. AUTHORITY

Each of us, whether we choose to instigate or not, is part of the conflict of creation. Simply put: we're either making stuff or we're not.

There are two sides to the conflict of creation:

The **Instigator** and **Authority**.

The Instigator seeks to alter the status quo, to change direction, and to create without permission. Authority seeks to maintain the status quo, to continue in the same direction, and to dictate what should (and should not) be created.

The Instigator believes in potentialities. Authority believes in realities.

The Instigator is bold, confrontational, and sometimes foolhardy. Authority is cautious, compromisable, and always predictable.

The Instigator does things that are inadvisable. Authority decides what is advisable.

I do not present this dichotomy to say that one side is *right* and the other *wrong*.

Authority has its place; the structure and progression of society relies to a degree on consistency, rationality, and forward movement.

Conversely, for all the positive change the Instigator creates, he is still a disrupter and often breaks things.

I present this dichotomy simply to say you *must* choose between the two.

When it comes to the war of art, to the conflict of creativity, and the battle of creation, you are either *bringing something new into existence*, or you're *perpetuating the current system*.

You cannot create something new by maintaining the old.

Neither is intrinsically better than the other.

But they don't coexist.

Which will you choose?

THE INSTIGATOR

It is the nature of the Instigator to challenge authority.

Authority enforces the status quo. The Instigator disrupts the status quo.

Authority seeks to maintain, align, and hold things in place. The Instigator aims to change, tweak, disrupt and break things.

Authority gives you a map to follow. The Instigator draws the map.

Authority demands you listen. The Instigator challenges you to question.

Authority adds slides to the PowerPoint meeting. The Instigator cancels meetings.

Authority threatens. The Instigator serves.

Authority demands you show up on time and leave no earlier than the designated time. The Instigator is busy doing work that matters.

Authority, when creating policy, defers to the lowest common denominator. The Instigator doesn't know what a denominator is.

Authority yells. The Instigator laughs.

Authority hates the Instigator.

INTO THE RING

> "IN THE CLEARING STANDS A BOXER AND A FIGHTER BY HIS TRADE, AND HE CARRIES THE REMINDER OF EVERY GLOVE THAT LAID HIM DOWN OR CUT HIM."
>
> Simon and Garfunkel

Being an Instigator and applying the *Art of Instigating* to your life is hard work.

You *will* get hit.

Instigating takes time, effort, focus, energy, and thick skin. When you choose to instigate, you're stepping into the ring, and you better be able to take a beating and keep going.

For the boxer, success is the title belt.

Not everyone can be a boxer.

Not everyone can deal with the blows, setbacks and failures. It takes heart and it takes experience.

If you don't have the passion, you probably won't make it to the end of the round. If you don't get into the ring at all, you'll never win anything, let alone the title belt.

A boxer doesn't become world champion by hitting a heavy bag – he becomes world champion by getting in the ring, day in and day out, to take a beating and to give one.

If he never sets foot in the ring, the boxer is guaranteed one thing: never to succeed.

If you can't take a hit, *stay out of the ring.*

500

Still here?

That means you can take a hit – or you're willing to step into the ring to find out. That's a good thing: the person willing to take a hit often can.

And now that you're committed to dealing with the worst, it's a matter of time until you become the best.

> "500 FIGHTS. THAT'S THE NUMBER I FIGURED WHEN I WAS A KID. 500 STREET FIGHTS AND YOU CAN CONSIDER YOURSELF A LEGITIMATE TOUGH GUY. YOU NEED THEM FOR EXPERIENCE - TO DEVELOP LEATHER SKIN. SO I GOT STARTED. OF COURSE, ALONG THE WAY, YOU STOP THINKING ABOUT BEING TOUGH AND ALL THAT, IT STOPS BEING THE POINT; YOU GET PAST THE SILLINESS OF IT ALL. BUT THEN - *AFTER* - YOU REALIZE THAT'S WHAT YOU ARE."
>
> Knockaround Guys

The Instigator becomes world class by instigating.

Instigating, like anything else, is a practice. Like becoming a doctor, lawyer, architect, programmer, salesman, or boxer, you must do it, day in and day out, to become an expert; to become the best.

Where are you on your path to 500?

WINNING BIG

The benefit of being the Instigator is, while you will take hits (a lot of hits), when you win, you win big:

> ## "IT IS THE VENTURE CAPITALIST WHO INVESTED IN A SPECULATIVE COMPANY AND SOLD HIS STAKE TO UNIMAGINATIVE INVESTORS WHO IS THE BENEFICIARY OF THE BLACK SWAN, NOT THE "ME, TOO" INVESTORS."
>
> Black Swan

By entering the arena of the Instigator, you're exposed to limited downside (the pain and emotional bruises that come with starting, finishing, and shipping), but you open yourself up to unlimited upside (what Nassim Taleb describes as a positive Black Swan event).

The effective cost of writing a book is close to zero (you could do it for free if you borrow a friend's computer or write it at the library). And once you've put in your initial work and upfront capital, there is nothing but upside in the digital space.

What is that book worth once you ship? Let's say you publish through Amazon's Kindle Direct Publishing, where you can sell your book for a 70% royalty fee. If you set the price at $10 and sell 100 copies, you make $700.

Not bad for the person starting out.

What if you sold 1,000 copies? That's $7,000 in your pocket. What if you sold 10,000 copies? You've just banked $70,000, and you can consider yourself a legitimate tough guy.

Whether you sell one or 1,000,000 copies, it's all the same amount of upfront work and capital. The upside is enormous.

And every project, group, or company you choose to lead is like this: you, the Instigator, get the lion's share of the profit and upside. You receive the uneven distribution of wealth from your efforts.

The employee receives his daily wage, no more, no less. The employee signs up for *peace of mind*, and he is happy as long as he has the perceived security of a steady job.

The owner/employer must pay his employees, overhead, and other expenses. *The owner takes the entire burden of the operation onto his shoulders*. It's a brutal, terrifying proposition. The owner risks everything.

But, for the owner, when it hits, it hits big.

The owner takes a big risk and reaps the benefits (all upside profit) when it works out.

The Instigator understands that every project he starts (finishes and ships) puts him in the *owner* column.

The Instigator understands that safety and security are secondary to making an impact, hitting big, and winning big.

The Instigator would rather own the mine than work the mine.

It's not for everyone.

It doesn't have to be.

PART II :

BURN THE

BOAT

THE CONFLICT

Whether you recognize it or not, you're at war.

This is not a conventional war:

The battle lines change every day.

The Enemy is dangerous, conniving, and unreasonable.

Your allies aren't who you would expect, but they're more powerful than you realize.

The warzone is not your physical environment – although the physical environment can help (or hinder) your campaign.

The Enemy is not a person (it's nothing external at all).

And your allies are not your friends or family, nor are they the people in the cubicle next to you at work.

This is a war fought in the neural trenches of your brain.

You are fighting the daily battle for self-control so that you can bring your vision (book, blog, business, etc.) to life.

> "BATTLES FOR SELF-CONTROL ARE NOT DEFECTS OF PERSONALITY, NOR CAN THEY BE WON IN THE SENSE THAT THE FOE IS VANQUISHED. TO TAKE CONTROL OF OUR LIVES, WE NEED PERPETUAL VIGILANCE AND AN UNDERSTANDING OF THE ENEMY WITHIN."
>
> Mean Genes

The "enemy within" is the Army of Bad Habits you've accumulated over the years – building and expanding its empire one brain-map territory at a time.

Your allies, if you choose to call upon them, are the virtuous and productive thoughts you put into your mind; they will support you when you are weak, and help you expand your territory when you are strong.

And you are the **insurgent** because you **seek change**, you **desire improvement**, and you **want to build something of value**.

You are *outnumbered* and *outgunned*.

The enemy controls the majority of the territory and continues to expand, becoming stronger every day.

But greater enemies have been conquered.

All it took was someone with guts, ready to go to war.

Are you ready?

THE WARZONE

Your brain is composed of billions of neurons.

These neurons talk to each other and form complex networks, where they send signals back and forth to communicate important information. They're responsible for how the brain functions, how we experience touch, taste, and other senses; and – most importantly – how we experience pain and pleasure.

Everything we do affects the brain.

Whether we perform physical or mental actions, learn new movements for sport or play, or simply experience anything through our senses, we are changing the neural pathways in our brain.

> "THE BRAIN CHANGED ITS VERY STRUCTURE WITH EACH DIFFERENT ACTIVITY IT PERFORMED, PERFECTING ITS CIRCUITS SO IT WAS BETTER SUITED TO THE TASK AT HAND... THINKING, LEARNING, AND ACTING CAN TURN OUR GENES ON OR OFF, THUS SHAPING OUR BRAIN ANATOMY AND OUR BEHAVIOR..."
>
> The Brain That Changes Itself

The actions we perform more often, the movements we practice more consistently, and the senses we employ more frequently, begin to control more brain map territory.

Because there is only so much territory to go around, our brain is in a perpetual state of conflict.

If you're not vigilant, the Enemy will destroy you.

THE ENEMY DEFINED

Have you ever put off making a sales call for weeks at a time and focused on tweaking your product pitch instead? You know the Enemy.

Have you ever started writing the first chapter of your book, then shelved the project indefinitely? You know the Enemy.

Have you ever hit the snooze button a half dozen times instead of waking up early to start your creative work? You know the Enemy.

The Enemy is what keeps us from doing the work we know we need to do.

The Enemy is what sabotages a project near the finish line or before it even starts.

The Enemy is the negative self-talk propaganda in our heads and the Army of Bad Habits we've accumulated over the years.

For most of us, the **Enemy has a disproportionate amount of control over our actions.**

And the Enemy will stop at nothing to make sure your project fails.

PACIFICATION

Try as we might, we can't directly control our bad habits or tell them to stop (try and they will laugh at us all the way to another scrapped project).

The Army of Bad Habits takes commands from another source – a crusty, battle-scarred commander with thousands of years of combat experience.

I'm talking about the **brain stem**.

The brain stem controls essential functions like breathing and blood pressure. It tells us when we're thirsty or hungry, and it lets us know when we're happy or sad. The brain stem compels us to seek pleasure and avoid pain (fight or flight? Yeah, that's the brain stem).

The brain stem is the Commanding General of the Army of Bad Habits, and *it will stop at nothing to keep you from creating your life's work.*

Of course, this creates a dilemma: the same thing that causes us so much misery and strife, that keeps us from accomplishing our goals and that limits our ability to take on new and bigger challenges is the same thing that keeps us alive and that seeks to preserve us.

The brain stem, you see, does not want to destroy you – his existence depends on your survival.

The brain stem simply wants to pacify you.

He wants you alive, but he wants you sedated.

> ## "I REQUIRE ONLY THAT YOU KNEEL."
> 300

ENEMY CONTROL

Every time we repeat a bad habit, the Enemy gains more control over brain map territory. With every repeated negative behavior, the Enemy territory expands and its neural trench network strengthens.

The reason the Army of Bad Habits controls so much brain map territory is because **we've lost the habit of starting**. The habit of starting has been ground out of us, and in its place we developed the **habit of hiding**.

> ## "IF WE STOP EXERCISING OUR MENTAL SKILLS, WE DO NOT JUST FORGET THEM: THE BRAIN MAP SPACE FOR THOSE SKILLS IS TURNED OVER TO THE SKILLS WE PRACTICE INSTEAD."
> The Brain That Changes Itself

For years, society has helped reinforce this habit of hiding; we discipline the child for not following directions; we form groups and cliques early in life and laugh at the outliers (and we do this through adulthood); we deride the employee who asks "why" instead of answering "how high."

It's not hard to see why most people don't instigate.

They lost the **habit of starting** years ago.

The habit of hiding is costing us our *happiness*, our *success*, and any chance at *living our purpose*.

The *Art of Instigating* **hinges** on redeveloping the habit of starting.

Developing the **habit of starting** is the first step to mastering the *Art of Instigating*.

Ignore it and everything you start will fail.

THE BRAIN MAP INSURGENT

Because you cannot simply destroy the leader of the Enemy, nor combat the Army of Bad Habits directly, you must learn other ways to undo its powerful control over your life.

You cannot win a conventional war with the Enemy; try and it will crush you. The Enemy is stronger than you ever could be.

> ## "WE CAN PERPETUALLY FIGHT AGAINST OUR GENES OR WE CAN OUTSMART THEM."
> Mean Genes

To beat the Enemy, you must respect its strength and attack its weakness.

You must fight an unconventional war – *a guerilla war*.

You must engage the enemy indirectly through subterfuge.

You must fight a protracted war and drain the Enemy of the will to fight.

In short, **you must fight as a *Brain Map Insurgent*.**

FIGHT LIKE AN INSURGENT

The *Brain Map Insurgent* knows where the Enemy is weakest, and precisely where to attack.

The Insurgent's most effective fighting techniques are:

1) **Discipline.**

The Enemy can't win a protracted war, and discipline is what allows us to fight that war.

The Enemy hates discipline more than anything else in the world. When you sit down to write *day in and day out*, the Enemy weakens. When you make sales calls *daily*, no matter what, the Enemy retreats.

When you go to work *every day*, you set in motion a certain power the Enemy can't defeat. *The Enemy cannot stop the disciplined person.*

2) **Concentration**.

The Enemy wants you to spread your forces thin and attack haphazardly. The Enemy fears you **focusing discriminately on one thing**; on one project; on one chapter; on one line. Concentrated effort on one thing dismantles the Enemy.

You've heard the idiom about the woodpecker pecking a million trees one time, or pecking one tree a million times. You know the result.

We should go about writing, building, or creating the same way we cut bread – at knife point.

3) Audacity.

The Enemy hates major commitments, virtuous goals, and ambitious struggles.

Audacity is acting with boldness and passion. It's about starting before you're ready. **It's about doing the big stupid thing people might laugh at.** It's about saying "why not" and going for it.

> ## "WHATEVER YOU CAN DO OR DREAM YOU CAN, BEGIN IT. BOLDNESS HAS GENIUS, POWER AND MAGIC IN IT."
> Goethe

TAKING BACK TERRAIN

To take back brain map territory, we must overcome a deeply entrenched Enemy.

By applying the techniques in the previous chapter – *Discipline, Concentration*, and *Audacity* – we beat back the Enemy, inch by inch, one territory at a time.

More importantly, as we consistently apply these fighting techniques, what we're really doing is developing the **habit of starting**.

By developing the habit of starting – *of going to work every day, of creating every day, of finishing and shipping every day* – we improve our ability to fight back against the Enemy.

Once we develop the habit of starting, instead of struggling for inches of territory, we reconquer entire neural networks with ease.

Here is how you apply the fighting techniques in the last chapter to the greatest effect (and create the habit of starting):

1) Mass forces at the weakest Enemy point

Don't try to regain control over every territory at once (i.e. don't try to overcome all your bad habits at once). It won't happen.

You'll lose focus and the Army of Bad Habits will crush you.

Start small.

Focus on one specific area instead. Use the power of **concentrated effort** at *one point* to break through enemy lines in order to gain a foothold before you move onto something else.

If you want to produce more creative work, **manipulate your environment** to make it easier.

This is where the Enemy is weakest – we have control over our physical environment and can use it to help us fight the Army of Bad Habits.

Get rid of distractions. Design your office space with the sole intent of creation and nothing else. Turn off the internet. Keep your phone in another room when you begin working. When you enter your office to work (whether your office is a coffee shop, a room in your house, or a corner office downtown), you are shut off from the rest of the world. Understand that. And make others understand it as well.

For the first few weeks, focus all your effort on getting control of this territory before moving on to something else.

2) Fight a protracted war

The only way to break through Enemy lines and expand friendly territory is through **consistent, daily action** over the course of three to six weeks. That's right, 21 to 42 days:

> **"THE SAME AMOUNT OF TIME IT TAKES FOR NEWLY BORN NEURONS IN THE HIPPOCAMPUS TO MATURE, EXTEND THEIR PROJECTIONS, AND CONNECT WITH OTHER NEURONS."**
> The Brain that Changes Itself

In other words, it takes three to six weeks to develop new muscle memory.

After the third week it doesn't mean the new muscle memory has become effortless habit. It simply means you've developed strong synapse connections, allowing you to more easily repeat the activity.

So stay **consistent**, even beyond those first three weeks. Remember: *the Enemy can't win a protracted war.*

3) Expand territorially

Brain maps are topographical, meaning the portions of the body's surface that are close together are mapped close together in the brain.

Similarly, when we perform an action that requires multiple motor movements (or multiple sensory inputs), the brain maps this *composite* skill as its *own map*. Running, for example, requires multiple inputs from various body parts, and the composite action is mapped locally on the brain.

> ## "ANIMALS EXPOSED TO A COMPLEX PATTERN, SUCH AS A MELODY OF SIX TONES, WILL NOT SIMPLY LINK TOGETHER SIX DIFFERENT MAP REGIONS BUT WILL DEVELOP A REGION THAT ENCODES THE *ENTIRE* MELODY."
>
> The Brain that Changes Itself

You can apply this knowledge by building good habits on top of other good habits.

Have you already created a habit out of waking up early? Expand on this good habit by sitting down for 10 minutes to write before work. Your brain will begin associating early rising with writing, and because a portion of the good habit already exists, it's much easier to develop more good habits on top of this one.

After 21 to 42 days, when the action becomes almost automatic, expand topographically again. For example, increase the amount of time you spend writing in the morning. Or focus on a specific output: like 1 page per morning session.

Slowly build your good habits and leverage the plasticity of the brain to make habit creation easy.

THE ENABLER OF THE ENEMY

A word of warning: your friends, family, and coworkers are not your allies *by default*.

In fact, while they may support your work outwardly, they are often times *indirect enablers of the enemy*.

In a study conducted by Emmanuelle Zech and Bernard Rime at the University of Louvain in Belgium, a group of participants were asked to describe their worst, most upsetting emotional event in their life. One group was told to talk about it with a supportive person; the other group was asked to talk to another person about a regular, boring, uneventful day (no focus on the trauma – just discussion about a mundane day). Their emotional well-being was measured by questionnaires, before and after the experiment. [**59 Seconds**]

Based on conventional self-help theory, you would expect the group that talked about their trauma to have higher emotional well-being, right?

While the group that discussed the traumatic event reported saying they felt better, the questionnaires showed no change to happiness or well-being. Their emotional well-being was no different than the control group that talked about a boring old day.

Why does this enable the enemy?

Because, while we're busy talking about our pains, no real progress of any kind is actually being made.

The Enemy has effectively **distracted** us.

The Enemy wants to keep us **occupied**, because if we're occupied, we can't write the book we want to write, build the business we want to build, or create the art we want to create.

If we're occupied discussing our difficulties with other people, we're not bringing our project to life.

As long as we stay occupied doing things that don't matter, that don't produce results, the Enemy is happy. The enemy wins.

Don't let the enemy use your friends and family against you.

Avoid distraction.

Focus on doing good work.

YOUR ALLIES

So if your friends, family and coworkers aren't your allies, who are?

Your allies in the war on the Enemy are the virtuous and thought provoking ideas you put into your head. You can do this through reading intellectually challenging literature or through powerful, uplifting conversation.

*note: *In this regard, your friends and family can be your allies, but only if they propel your thinking to new heights (not occupy your time with time-wasting distractions).*

A caveat: your allies can't do the work for you; *they simply improve your ability to fight.*

Don't expect that reading great source material will write your book for you. Nor should you expect that a brilliant conversation with your friend will create the million dollar business by itself.

You must still do the work.

Your allies simply help in their own ways.

Some tips on using your allies to help you fight the good fight:

1) **Read daily**

To produce, you need a consistent flow of new material from which to pull and create. Reading daily is something entirely in your control, so avoid wasting time on time-wasters (most magazines). Choose your content wisely.

Don't be afraid to reread great material.

> **"IT IS A GOOD RULE AFTER READING A NEW BOOK, NEVER TO ALLOW YOURSELF ANOTHER NEW ONE TILL YOU HAVE READ AN OLD ONE IN BETWEEN."**
> C.S. Lewis

2) Converse and associate with people above your current intellectual threshold

> **"YOU ARE THE AVERAGE OF THE FIVE PEOPLE YOU SPEND THE MOST TIME WITH."**
> Jim Rohn

You've most likely heard some variation of that quote at some point in your life.

And, if you take a hard look at your own life, it's most likely that this statement – as painful as it is to admit to ourselves – is true.

If you're surrounding yourself with slow, superficial thinkers, they will most certainly drag you down to their level.

Once you've gotten rid of the people dragging you down, seek out people growing and expanding like you (I suggest leveraging the internet for this – why restrict ourselves to our physical geography when we have the world at our fingertips?)

3) **Do work**

Noticing a trend?

Nothing gets done unless *you* start.

No amount of books, or money, or friends, or circumstance, or luck will write your book, build your business, or lead your organization.

You are the essential piece.

Get to work.

[INTERLUDE]

A PAUSE IN BATTLE

TAKE A KNEE

You're in the thick of it now.

I've thrown a lot at you and it's especially important at times like this, when we're overwhelmed with information, to take a knee, reflect, and regroup.

Up to this point, we've covered:

Part 1 – Hit the Shore

- A brief overview of the Art of Instigating (*a method and practice for creating your life's work*)
- What it means to instigate (*to create something without permission*)
- The stages of instigating (*start, finish, ship*)
- What's at stake (*everything*)
- What's REALLY at stake (*your freedom*)
- The dichotomy of creation (*Instigator vs Authority*)
- The downside of being an Instigator (*you will get hit*)
- The upside of being an Instigator (*when you win, you win big*)

Part 2 – Burn the Boat

- The conflict (*the warfare of creativity*)
- The warzone (*the neural trenches in your brain*)
- The Enemy (*Army of Bad Habits commanded by the brain stem*)
- The Insurgent (*that's you*)

- How to fight and **beat** the enemy (*discipline, concentration, audacity*)
- The most effective way to take back Enemy held terrain, i.e. create new, positive habits (*mass forces at the weakest Enemy point, fight a protracted war, expand territorially*)
- A warning for all Instigators (*your friends and family aren't your allies by default*)
- The real allies in your fight against the Enemy (*intellectual books, intellectual conversation, your own work*)

Interlude – A Pause in Battle

That's what we're doing right now – reflecting and regrouping.

And now that we've taken note of where we started and how far we've come, it's time to put this information to work.

Part 3 will help motivate you to **do the work** – which, sure enough, is where we most often fail.

You already know the secrets.

You know the techniques.

If you've been paying attention, you know what it means to be an Instigator, and you understand what it takes to master the *Art of Instigating*.

Now: it's time to *put your helmet back on*, *move out*, and **get to work**.

PART III :

TAKE THE

BEACH

[RATED R]

BUILDING EMPIRES

Rome wasn't built in a day, nor was it built with one great idea and a moment of youthful enthusiasm.

Rome was built – like every empire – one small action at a time.

And like every empire, the final result is much different than the original idea.

So if you're not sure where to start, **start anyway**.

Take one small action today; and then take another small action tomorrow; and another one after that.

Why?

Because **you don't need to have it all figured out before you start.** Things change. Your plan will change. Your empire will always end up different than you anticipated.

But taking action now – that is something you must do, because actions repeated consistently over time create habit, and habit creates momentum, and momentum can make us or bury us.

If you don't write tonight, nothing happens. If you don't write tomorrow, same thing, nothing happens. There is no dramatic, immediate effect to doing nothing.

And a year from now, you'll reap exactly what you sowed.

But if you **do** write tonight, and tomorrow, and every day for the next year, pretty soon you'll have enough for a book – and then enough for a series – and, eventually, enough for a 'best of' collection.

*By writing every day, you'll get your 500 fights, and you'll get passed the silliness of **trying** to be a writer and you'll actually **be** one.*

The point is this: *you'll never complete a project by waiting until tomorrow.* And don't try to fool yourself into thinking you'll catch up this weekend (you won't). Don't worry about tomorrow – it doesn't exist, not to you, not when you're staring at an empty page.

Building an empire successfully requires the *habit of starting*, and it begins with action *right now*.

The spark of enthusiasm at the beginning of a quest is essential, but it is the **grit** and **persistence** of daily action that builds empires.

Start creating – immediately: never end a day until you've added another stone, brick, or pillar to your empire.

OVERCOMING THE KILLER OF PROJECTS

The hidden fear of every Instigator is **fear of exposure.**

Every Instigator experiences this same fear.

From the moment he puts pen to paper to begin, to the heart pounding ship date, **fear of exposure threatens the completion of every great project.**

Every Instigator wonders whether his work is *good enough*, how the tribe will react, and whether he'll be jeered and criticized (or worse, laughed at).

This (naturally) leads to thoughts of scrapping the project entirely, procrastinating in the name of perfection, and avoiding the publish button at all costs.

Every one of these reactions is merely a way to avoid finishing, to avoid shipping, and, ultimately, to **avoid the pain of standing out.**

If you're going through this same struggle right now, STOP. You're killing yourself (and your project) for no reason. Here's the thing:

There is no angry group of critics waiting to disrespect your work.

There are no mobs of people waiting to judge you when you publish.

While you stress out over making it "perfect" and wonder if your tribe will hate you, you're missing this glaring fact:

*Your tribe **doesn't exist.***

> "THERE IS NO TRIBE. THAT GANG OR POSSE THAT WE IMAGINE IS SUSTAINING US BY THE BONDS WE SHARE IS IN FACT A CONGLOMERATION OF INDIVIDUALS WHO ARE JUST AS FUCKED UP AS WE ARE AND JUST AS TERRIFIED. EACH INDIVIDUAL IS SO CAUGHT UP IN HIS OWN BULLSHIT THAT HE DOESN'T HAVE TWO SECONDS TO WORRY ABOUT YOURS OR MINE, OR TO REJECT OR DIMINISH US BECAUSE OF IT."
>
> Turning Pro

Stop worrying about this imaginary group of people watching you. Don't stress about the possibility of negative reviews of your product.

All you have control over is your work.

Do it every day.

Finish your product and push it out to the market.

F*** the tribe.

BIG STUPID PLANS

Here is what you must do:

Write your big stupid book, build your big stupid business, or start your big stupid blog.

Start your big stupid organization with its big stupid goal, and get after it with all the big stupid *intensity* and big stupid *ambition* of someone who just doesn't understand what a prudent course of action is.

Why?

Because, as an instigator, everything you do will be "big stupid."

If it wasn't, it would be prudent; if it was prudent, it would be advisable; if it was advisable, *Authority* would have already ordered it done.

And remember: your project will always be stupid for the few people who think it's stupid (*Authority*).

But for the rest of us, we think it's great.

CLOSE WITH AND DESTROY THE ENEMY

"GRENDEL IS NO BRAVER, NO STRONGER

THAN I AM! I COULD KILL HIM WITH MY SWORD;
I SHALL NOT,

EASY AS IT WOULD BE. THIS FIEND IS A BOLD

AND FAMOUS FIGHTER, BUT HIS CLAWS AND TEETH...

BEATING AT MY SWORD BLADE, WOULD BE HELPLESS.
I WILL MEET HIM

WITH MY HANDS EMPTY - UNLESS HIS HEART

FAILS HIM, SEEING A SOLDIER WAITING

WEAPONLESS, UNAFRAID. LET GOD IN HIS WISDOM

EXTEND HIS HAND WHERE HE WILLS, REWARD

WHOM HE CHOOSES!"

Beowulf

You don't need a weapon to close with and destroy the Enemy.

Sure, Beowulf was a warrior badass, but when it comes to writing, building a business, creating your blog, or starting a gang, you *ARE* Beowulf.

Grendel represents all of our fears: fear of uncertainty, exposure, commitment; fear of starting, finishing, and shipping; fear of failing and fear of winning.

These fears manifest in many forms: writers block, scrapping projects, procrastination (or, for Beowulf, a big ass monster).

But remember this: while the Enemy is a bold and famous fighter, *he is no braver and no stronger than you.*

While it would be nice to be born into wealth, or into the right family; to be born the right height, with the right hair and the right complexion; or to have the right connections, the right opportunities and the right timing; you don't need these weapons to make something incredible – easy as it would be.

You don't need anything more than your **desire**, your **commitment**, and your **passion** to beat the Enemy.

Meet the Enemy *unafraid* and *weaponless*; meet the Enemy with your bare hands, with the *grit* and *determination* of a warrior.

Meet the Enemy *as you are* and ***create your life's work.***

ALL IN

493 years ago, Cortez and an army of 600 soldiers landed on the shores of Central America and conquered an empire of over 5 million people.

His first order upon landing: **destroy the ships.**

Cortez knew if he kept the ships seaworthy, the men would believe they could escape if things got bad. By destroying the ships, Cortez removed "escape" from the equation.

It was, quite literally, do or die.

Maybe we have to destroy the ships in our own lives.

If you have that gut feeling to start something; that desire that never fades (the one that beats you up for not writing enough pages); if you know deep down *this is it* —you were *made for this*...

Then *hit the shore, burn the boat,* and *take the beach.*

When you consciously go beyond *wanting* to *choosing*, you've **hit the shore.**

When you *commit*, in the face of The Enemy, to pursue what you want no matter the cost, you **burn the boat.**

And when you start chipping away at the material and sit down every day in order to finish and ship your product, you **take the beach.**

This type of commitment is frightening; it's not for everyone.

And that's why we need you to instigate now more than ever.

I told you the *Art of Instigating* was simple.

I never said it was easy.

READY.

Are you ready to do the work, day in and day out?

Are you ready to hit the shore, burn the boat, and take the beach?

Are you ready to fail?

Good, then you understand the *Art of Instigating*, now all you have to do is apply it.

Go – create your life's work.

And let me know when you do – I want to see it.

> *"LIFE IS AN OPPORTUNITY, BENEFIT FROM IT.*
>
> *LIFE IS BEAUTY, ADMIRE IT.*
>
> *LIFE IS A DREAM, REALIZE IT.*
>
> *LIFE IS A CHALLENGE, MEET IT...*
>
> *LIFE IS LIFE, FIGHT FOR IT."*

Mother Teresa

INDEX / RESOURCES

In chronological order of appearance
(with links for your convenience):

SOURCES OF INSPIRATION

A list of all the ideas and people, past and present, that have made an impact and inspired this eBook: Seth Godin (for his ideas on starting, shipping and poking the box), Steven Pressfield (for his ideas on the Resistance and the War of Art), Paulo Coelho (for his lessons on being a warrior of the light), Austin Kleon (because originality is a remix), Maxwell Maltz (for some of the best psychological research ever put into one book), C.S. Lewis (for his concise and powerful writing – I aspire to the same), Nassim Taleb (possibly the greatest philosopher of our time), and everyone else who was quoted/cited in this book; Dan (for giving my writing meaning), Bill (living as an instigator from day 1), Joe (because the world needs whatever crazy thing you're going to make), Mary (doing art the right way), Kathy (for helping me write my first book in 1st grade), Christy (for challenging me on all my beliefs and helping me gain clarity), Mom (for thinking I'm handsome), Dad (for thinking I'm crazy), Bob, Aaron, Chris, Alan, Derek (for supporting my crazy ideas)…oh, and the jump sequence from the movie Sunshine; there is no more intense scene in any movie ever; I tried to craft this eBook with the same energy and same intensity [**http://www.youtube.com/watch ?v=clG_1sqOsBs**]; makes more sense in context – so watch the whole movie.

ABOUT THE AUTHOR

Tom Morkes is an author, investor, and professional instigator.

Tom graduated from the United States Military Academy at West Point, NY with a double major in Russian (Prevyet!) and Human Geography (he can read people). He is an Iraq War veteran and has lead troops in combat.

And, for a while, he was paid to jump out of helicopters.

During his years of active duty military service, Tom has learned no more important lesson than this: **people need you to instigate.**

Every team is waiting for someone to take point, to lead, to be the first to jump out of the helicopter.

People are waiting; the question is, are you ready and willing to **instigate**?

You can connect with Tom **http://tommorkes.com/connect/**
Find out more about him: **http://tommorkes.com/about/**
Or just send an email to:
tom@tommorkes.com

You can read more of Tom's writing at:
http://tommorkes.com